SLEEPER

SCRIBNER

First published in Great Britain by Scribner, an imprint of Simon &
Schuster UK Ltd, 2021

A CBS COMPANY

1 3 5 7 9 10 8 6 4 2
Simon & Schuster UK Ltd
1st Floor
222 Gray's Inn Road
London WC1X 8HB

www.simonandschuster.co.uk
www.simonandschuster.com.au
www.simonandschuster.co.in

Simon & Schuster Australia, Sydney
Simon & Schuster India, New Delhi

A CIP catalogue record for this book is available from the British Library

Trade Paperback ISBN: 978-1-4711-9497-9
eBook ISBN: 978-1-4711-9498-6

Written by Jed Mercurio and Prasanna Puwanarajah
Illustrated by Coke Navarro

# SLEEPER

## BOOK 1

WRITTEN BY
JED MERCURIO AND PRASANNA PUWANARAJAH

ILLUSTRATED BY
COKE NAVARRO

SCRIBNER

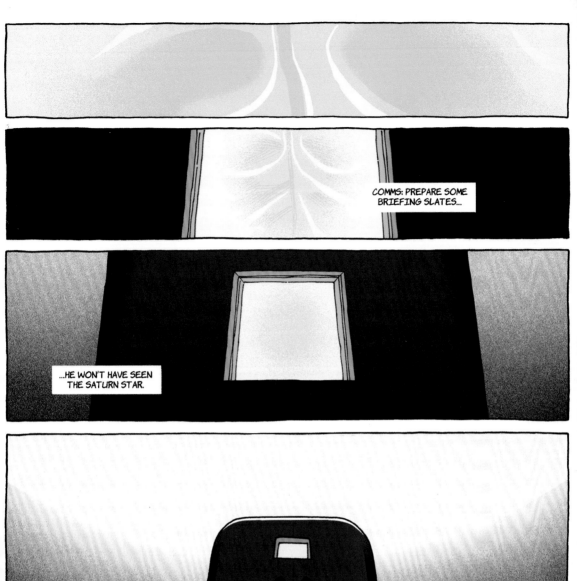

COMMS: PREPARE SOME BRIEFING SLATES...

...HE WON'T HAVE SEEN THE SATURN STAR.

AND LET'S RUN HAZARD PROTOCOLS TO THE LETTER, PEOPLE...

**CHAPTER 1**

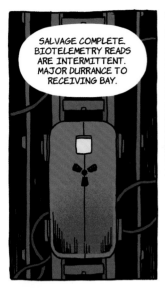

SALVAGE COMPLETE. BIOTELEMETRY READS ARE INTERMITTENT. MAJOR DURRANCE TO RECEIVING BAY.

LET'S KEEP HIM FROM BECOMING AGITATED.

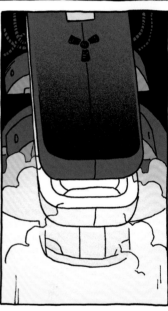

DESIGNATION?

DS-5.

REPORTING TO LUNAR BASE HADLEY FOR DECOMMISSIONING.

STEADY MARSHAL...

YOU'RE NOT ON THE MOON.

THE GRAVITY IN THIS SPACE IS FLUCTUATING. 6.47M/S² REGISTERED MINIMUM. CAUSE UNKNOWN.

I GOT THE CAUSE: A GLITCHY, SHITTY OLD STATION.

YOU DON'T NEED THE GUARDS.

YOU KNOW I DO.

IF YOU DID, YOU WOULD HAVE NEEDED THEM BY NOW.

AND SEVEN BODY BAGS...

I SAW A PLANET LIKE THIS IN THE GROOMBRIDGE TRANSIT...

...IT WAS A LAWLESS WORLD. YOU COULD SEE THE FIRES FROM SPACE.

YOU'RE BACK IN THE SOLAR SYSTEM.

I WAS TASKED TO LUNAR BASE HADLEY FOR DECOMMISSIONING. THAT IS NOT EARTH'S MOON.

WE'VE MOVED.

WE PROJECTED YOUR REQUIREMENT FOR EVIDENCE.

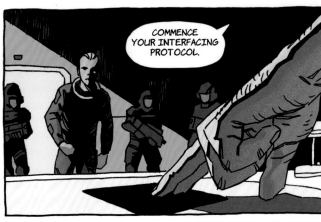

COMMENCE YOUR INTERFACING PROTOCOL.

FIVE YEARS AGO, AN INTERNATIONAL PROJECT...

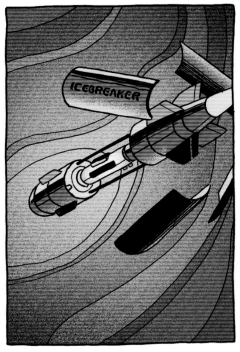

ICEBREAKER

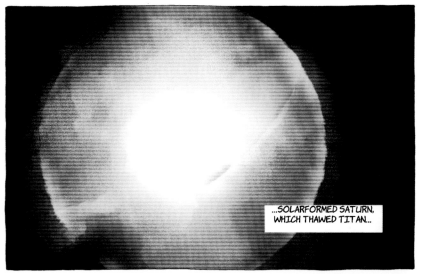

...SOLARFORMED SATURN, WHICH THAWED TITAN...

...TO MINE A FUEL. TITAN GREEN. MAKES URANIUM LOOK LIKE A TWIGLIT FIRE.

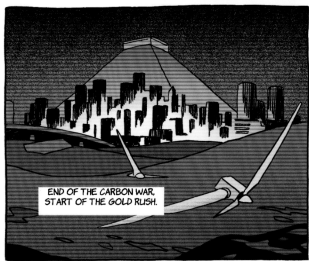

END OF THE CARBON WAR, START OF THE GOLD RUSH.

WE THOUGHT WE'D LOSE THE RINGS. THERE WERE PROTESTS.

DS-5, DO YOU SUBMIT TO FORMAL DECOMMISSIONING AND SALVAGE?

AFFIRMATIVE.

COMMENCE PROTOCOL.

COMMENCING TERMINATION?

DO IT.

ON BEHALF OF A GRATEFUL PLANET...

...WE THANK YOU FOR YOUR SERVICE.

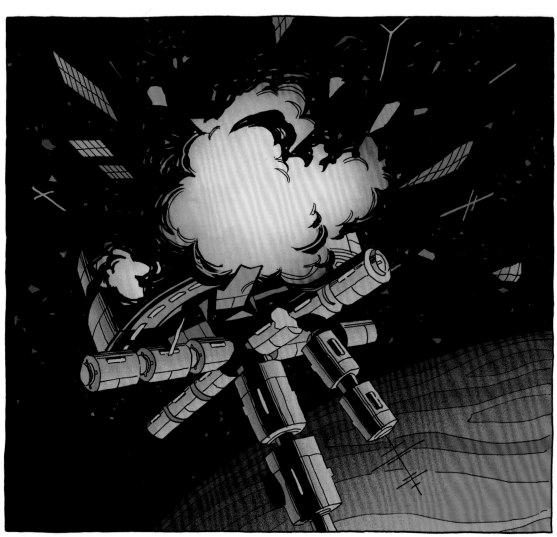

WHAT DID YOU DO?

PERPETRATOR UNKNOWN.

LAUNCH

DIVERGENT ON ALL THREE AXES. G-LOC IMMINENT. ENGAGE YOUR HARNESS!

HATCH FAILURE

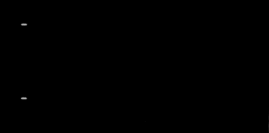

/Breathing_

-

-

-

NITROGEN: 94.2%
METHANE: 5.65%
HYDROGEN: 0.099%
ETHANE: T
DIACETYLENE: T
METHYLACETYLENE: T
ACETYLENE: T
PROPANE: T

/Adjusting Respiratory
Substrate Profile_

/Initialising_

Emergency System Reboot
/DS-5: New crime detected_
398345-8 ISS-HOUSTON

CRIME CODE_92:

/UNLAWFUL DESTRUCTION OF FEDERAL PROPERTY_

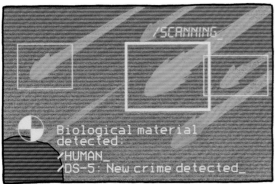

/SCANNING_

Biological material detected:
/HUMAN_
/DS-5: New crime detected_

CRIME CODE_01:

/MURDER_

_YO_J93Q :E-2O\

CHAPTER 2

SABOTAGE ON BOARD
ISS HOUSTON

EXPLOSION ABOARD ISS HOUSTON.
Titan Green supplies threatened.

...TRAGIC LOSS OF 83 LIVES, MANY OF WHOM WERE EMPLOYEES OF TEXONSATURN.

THIS AFTERNOON PRESIDENT GARDNER DECLARED A STATE OF EMERGENCY AND MANY GLOBAL LEADERS HAVE...

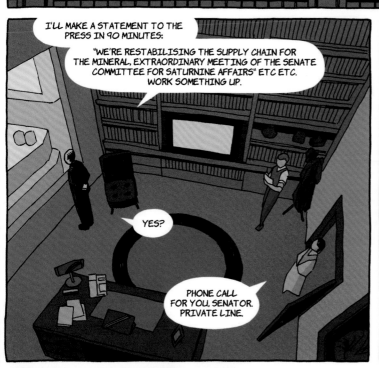

I'LL MAKE A STATEMENT TO THE PRESS IN 90 MINUTES:

"WE'RE RESTABILISING THE SUPPLY CHAIN FOR THE MINERAL, EXTRAORDINARY MEETING OF THE SENATE COMMITTEE FOR SATURNINE AFFAIRS" ETC ETC. WORK SOMETHING UP.

YES?

PHONE CALL FOR YOU, SENATOR. PRIVATE LINE.

FONSECA.

WE'RE REQUESTING OPERATIONAL JURISDICTION OVER SATURNINE LAW ENFORCEMENT. WE'VE GOT AN OPERATIVE ON TITAN WHO ESCAPED THE ISS EXPLOSION.

HOW'S THAT POSSIBLE... NOTHING'S SURVIVING THAT...

WHO DID YOU SAY YOU WERE?

THIS IS COLONEL REETU GHAVRI IN THE OFFICE OF THE OFF-WORLD MARSHAL. WE'RE STATIONED OUT OF...

I'VE HEARD OF YOU GUYS. SHIT.

SO WHAT YOU'RE SAYING IS THIS OPERATIVE IS...

HE'S A SLEEPER.

HE'S AN AUTONOMOUS UNIT. THEY HAVE TO BE THAT FAR OUT. THEY INVESTIGATE FACTS, COLLATE THEM, AND HUNT MORE FACTS. RELENTLESSLY.

LEAVE IT TO US. HE'LL FIND OUT WHO DID THIS, AND WHY...

GREAT.

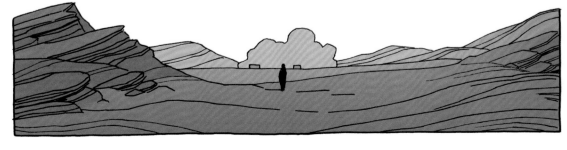

26

HOLD YOUR POSITION. DO NOT MOVE OR YOU WILL BE FIRED UPON. BRYCE, SHERIFF OF TITAN. IDENTIFY YOURSELF.

DESIGNATION DS-5.

SIR, I NEED YOU TO STEP INTO THE VEHICLE, YOU'LL FREEZE. YOU'RE FROZEN.

WHAT THE FUCK IS THIS, WHERE'S HIS EVA SUIT?

BOSS!

MOVE!

BY AUTHORITY OF THE OFFICE OF THE OFF-WORLD MARSHAL, I HEREBY CLAIM JURISDICTION OVER CASE 398345-B: THE DESTRUCTION OF THE SPACE STATION ISS HOUSTON AND THE MURDER OF 83 PERSONS MISSING PRESUMED DEAD.

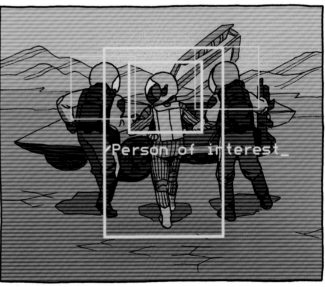

HE'S HUMAN... BUT HE AIN'T.

HOW CAN HE BE A HUMAN? HIS CORE TEMPERATURE WAS MINUS 15 CELSIUS.

HE COULD BE 115 CELSIUS. THAT'S A FUCKING SLEEPER WE GOT IN THERE.

WHEN I WAS A KID WE USED TO HEAR ABOUT THESE WEIRD SPACE COWBOYS WHO COULD BREATHE WHATEVER - SULPHUR AND SHIT - AND THEY TRAVELLED AROUND THE GALAXY CATCHING OUTLAWS.

AROUND THE GALAXY? ARE YOU ON CRACK?

I'M TELLING YOU! THESE THINGS SHIT BITUMEN! AND BETWEEN THEIR LEGS, THEY SAY IT'S LIKE A BARBIE.

QUIT IT. FOCUS.

AS THE SOLE SURVIVOR OF A MAJOR IN-ORBIT DISASTER, YOU'RE GONNA BE HIGH ON MY LIST OF "TERRORISTS WHO MIGHT HAVE TORCHED THE ISS HOUSTON", RIGHT?

HAVE YOU ANALYSED THE SALVAGE FRAGMENTS FROM ISS HOUSTON?

OKAY. I GET IT. YOU'RE THE SWINGING DICK AND WE'RE THE LOCAL PD.

GIVE ME ONE GOOD REASON TO HAND THIS CASE OVER TO YOU.

SHIT! CAN HE SEE US?

WAIT, DO YOU EXIST? DO SLEEPERS EXIST?

MITCHELL, SHUT IT!

DO YOU?

IF YOU'RE GOING TO HOLD ME YOU NEED THE AUTHORISATION OF THE DEPARTMENT OF DEEP SPACE IN WASHINGTON. OTHERWISE I AM AUTHORISED TO DO WHAT I NEED TO DO... TO NOT BE HELD.

I KNOW WHAT YOU ARE. YOU DON'T INTIMIDATE ME...

FREAK.

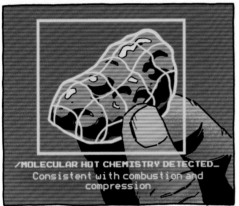

/MOLECULAR HOT CHEMISTRY DETECTED_
Consistent with combustion and
compression

ISS HOUSTON DIDN'T EXPLODE.

IT WAS CRUSHED.

WHO ADMINISTERED THE STATION ISS HOUSTON?

TEXONSATURN. THE TITAN GREEN CORPORATION.

NOT VERY WELL BRIEFED FOR "THE COP WITH JURISDICTION" ARE YOU?

I COMMANDEER YOUR HOLSTER.

OH WAIT, YOU'RE NO COP. YOU'RE A THUMB DRIVE WITH SKIN.

IT'S GOING TO STEAL A VEHICLE!

LASSITER, TAKE HIM!

FUCK YOU, BOSS, YOU TAKE HIM.

DAMN IT! FALL BACK!

STAND YOUR MEN DOWN. IF YOU WANT THEM TO LIVE.

33

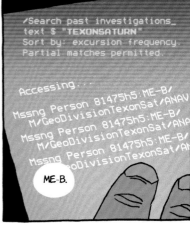

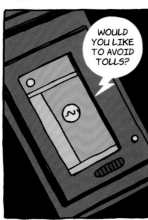

10 March 2378

Carsten Horvath
https://www.washingtonpost.com/travel/CHorvath/blog/Titan_thegreengoldrush.en
The Green Gold Rush

I never thought I'd say it: the System is interested in Titan again. I'm going to do that really annoying thing now: I went there before it was cool, about 20 years ago. Just before college when, typically addled with the delusion that our clichés weren't clichés because they were ours, a couple of friends and I went on an Interplanet ticket trip to the places that no one else wanted to go to, mainly so we could revel in our own irony. Top of the list – the Anchorage of the Solar System, the "bumfuck nowhere" to end them all – was Titan. Intergalactically renowned moonhole. "Do they even have Icomms?" I remember my mother asking me. "No", I replied teenagedly. "They just shout to Earth really loudly."

Like all great shitholes, the one good thing about Titan was the view looking up. (Not anymore, but the coffee's great. Welcome, humans.) I'm one of those irritating smugs who remembers the view of the Rings from low Titan orbit and who likes to tell everyone that. I remember the way it was never really night there: the way light did an extraordinary dance about those rings like a space ocean was somehow pulling it around. Icebreaker really was an act of mutilation, and I say that with a 20-year-old memory fresh in my mind of the rings as seen from Titan, but also as someone who hasn't switched off a light in 5 years. We don't deserve the remaining ring fragments, having swapped the most beautiful thing in our universe for a decent espresso in Downtown Anavra and a slightly thawed moon.

As they say in the lofty Washington and Houston circles of The Titan Green Project: you need a bit of heat to make a moon cool again. But it so wasn't cool back then. Off we went in our hairshirts, me and my two buddies. Mars, Ceres (don't believe what anyone tells you: it's still a great party world), Ganymede with its retro-lunar feels, Europa (underrated, artistic, industrial), and Titan (shithole). We took the TSI, which in those days was pretty basic. The food was the kind you added hot water to, which of course we a) relished as great travel-anecdote fodder and b) puked up. When we landed at Anavra, it didn't disappoint in its overwhelming, unburnished disappointment. It really was a dive. Every EVA suit stank. Icey desert towns, Pripyat-style abandonment, hydrocarbon tumbleweed. The desolate, brutalist BullRing, once the home of the University of Anavra Bulldogs, now lay open to the atmosphere, its long-decayed AstroTurf quite literally now a field of the stars, the faded gold and white of the end zones like runic markings of an ancient civilisation. The Titan Senate building had lost its windows at that point, a Reichstag without a war, and a small tourist information bureau nearby had nothing whatsoever to say about Titan: the guy was shocked to see us, only able to offer information on how to leave.

The place reeked of old piss and unfulfilled promise. In every depowered hoarding and empty, see-through building you could feel the over-reach not of human hope but human largesse, an inescapable orbiting monument to the hubristic fall of deep-space capitalism were it not for the fact that it was kind of Stalinist in its blunt and wasteful physical expression. We so wanted Titan to be the one, didn't we? But didn't it just go the way of all such acts of species betterment: the first Titan settlement was an expression of who we actually were, not who we might be. Where we go in search of our next Enlightenment are the same places where we go in pursuit of the next dollar or fuck. The trash on Everest, the McDonald's at Tranquility. How desperate we must have been in that century-long war, plunderers back then on a scale unmatched since the Conquistadors, seeking the answer to the apparently unanswerable Carbon Question in the most inhospitable dump in the Solar System.

The single greatest failing of the species has been its overwhelming energy debt. We've never solved it, and for the centuries that followed the Carbon Crash we looked like we never would. Even now, it wasn't a solution we came up with; rather it arrived fully formed into our lives like an adult baby; the discovery of Titan Green is one that we made by accident. (Sorry Stanford, but it's true: you fluked it; and I'm not just saying that as a Berkeley Grad.) Years after we actually tried to find it, we blithely stumble upon the energy holy grail because some nerds went digging for their PhDs. Salvation of our species cometh from the nerd: whoever it was who was nerdy enough (yes we all know who, but go with) to restart the geological mapping of Titan at this point in its journey as an economic dangleberry of Earth must have had a life-length gap in their diary. That strange luck, and the fact that we're still working out its chemistry – and I'm no chemist but honestly? I thought we had that shit down – must make Titan Green the barn-find of all time. I love that our first thought was to burn a bit of it. We really aren't that far out of the caves.

But how many times have we been told: "it burns cleanly". "It's a clean fuel". "It's the God Chemical". Is anything clean? There are still bodies buried in the Hoover Dam. What were the chances that, in the vastness of travelled human space, in all those worlds around all those stars, we essentially found Eldorado in our own trashcan? But sure – we'll give it a shot to end a war.

So, Titan's on the map again. It used to be so uncool, not to mention cold. Hard to think of it now, as the lights burn all the day long, every kind of day, on every world we know, that we accidentally found the answer there, in *that* place, years later, long after we saw Titan for what it was: a burnt-out frontier of a lost gold rush.

EXCUSE ME OFFICER... I NEED YOU TO REMOVE YOUR HELMET, PLEASE, THIS IS A REGULATED INTERNAL FACILITY.

ARE YOU WITH THE INVESTIGATION?

ISS HOUSTON DISASTER

I NEED TO SEE ANY AND ALL FILES ON ISS HOUSTON.

I, UH... CAN I SEE AN UP-TO-DATE WARRANT?

THIS IS A MASS HOMICIDE. INTERPLANETARY FEDERAL JURISDICTION APPLIES, IN ACCORDANCE WITH IFJ CONSTITUTION, ARTICLES 17 THROUGH 19. WARRANTS NOT APPLICABLE.

I NEED TO SPEAK TO, UH... I NEED TO, UM...

WHO IS ME-B?

Password function disabled

TEXON SA ... N DRILL SITES

38

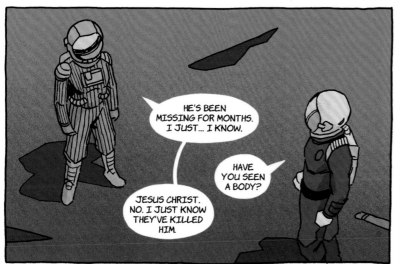

HE'S BEEN MISSING FOR MONTHS. I JUST... I KNOW.

HAVE YOU SEEN A BODY?

JESUS CHRIST. NO. I JUST KNOW THEY'VE KILLED HIM.

WHO HAS KILLED HIM?

TEXONSATURN. THE SATURNINE JURISDICTION... I DON'T KNOW. SOMEONE.

THEY SHUT THIS SITE DOWN YEARS AGO. HE CAME HERE THE DAY HE DISAPPEARED. NOW THEY'VE FILLED IN THE BOREHOLES. I DON'T KNOW IF HE'S STILL DOWN THERE...

I AM NOT TASKED TO FIND YOUR FATHER. PROBABILITY OF CASE CROSSOVER WITH PRIMARY INVESTIGATION IS IN THE ERROR MARGIN. I NEED MORE DATA, MS EL-BUSHRA.

DR EL-BUSHRA.

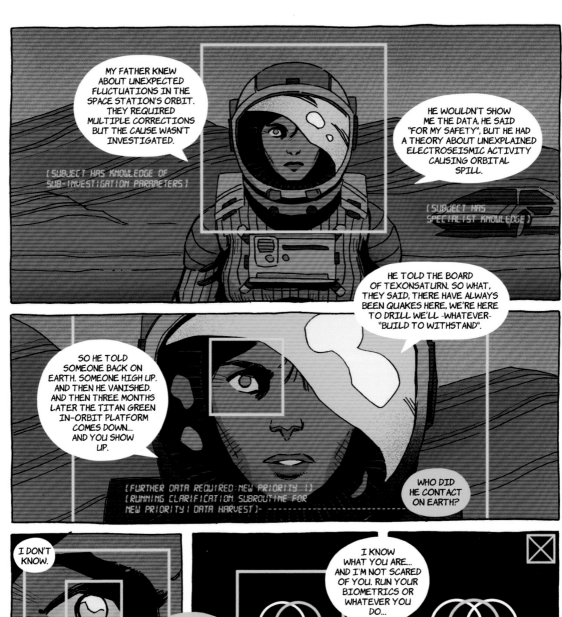

WE HAVE TO MOVE!

TAGGART...

44

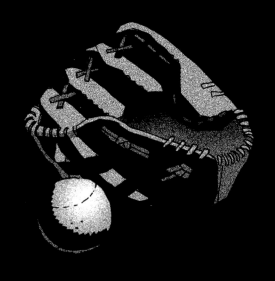

**CHAPTER 3**

MY PRESENCE HERE IS CLASSIFIED.

I WON'T TELL IF YOU DON'T.

YOU MAY NOT DIVULGE THIS INFORMATION REGARDLESS OF MY...

WOW. YOU'VE NOT MET MANY PEOPLE HAVE YOU?

I CHECKED THE TITAN RECORD. THERE'S NO ONE NAMED "TAGGART" ON THIS MOON...

"TAGGART" WAS A SPEECH AREA MALFUNCTION.

I WAS DUE TO BE DECOMMISSIONED BEFORE MALFUNCTION COMPROMISES PERFORMANCE.

WHAT HAPPENED WHEN I TOUCHED YOUR SKIN? WAS THAT A MALFUNCTION? IT FELT...

NO.
YOU EXPERIENCED MOMENTARY NEURAL FEEDBACK.

OF WHAT...?

EVERYTHING.

AFTER YOUR SLEEP CYCLE I WILL INVESTIGATE YOUR FATHER'S RESIDENCE FOR EVIDENCE. DO NOT ATTEMPT TO LEAVE THIS MOON.

WHY?

BECAUSE UNTIL I DETERMINE THAT YOU ARE A WITNESS, YOU ARE A SUSPECT.

I'M GOING TO BED. I'M SURE YOU WANT TO BE ALONE.

IT'S BETTER THAT WAY... IN CASE OF MALFUNCTION.

COLONEL, HE'S REPORTING IN!

WHAT'S THE HEADLINE?

"REPORTING A MAJOR MALFUNCTION. REQUESTING EVAC AND REPLACE."

WHAT'S THE MALFUNCTION?

HE CAN'T REMEMBER

THAT'S THE MALFUNCTION. HE CAN'T REMEMBER OR REPORT WHAT'S GONE WRONG. BUT HE'S INVESTIGATING THE ISS HOUSTON EXPLOSION. HOLDING HIS OWN. DATA DOWNLOAD IN PROGRE—

COLONEL! ABNORMAL ACTIVITY IN THE PARIETAL LOBES!

HAS HE... BEEN DREAMING?

UM...

IT'S NOT CLEAR YET, COLONEL. BUT HE'S AN OLD UNIT AND HE'S BEEN BREATHING THE AIR UP THERE...

UNDERSTOOD. TASK HIM TO CONTINUE INVESTIGATION.

FOR NOW.

GIVE ME A MINUTE.

WE MUST BEGIN.

THAT'S NOT RIGHT. THESE USED TO BE IN HIS BEDROOM.

ALL FROM MUM. ONE EVERY BIRTHDAY... EXCEPT THAT ONE. I DON'T REMEMBER THAT ONE...

THIS WAS HIS BIRTHDAY THIS YEAR. LAKE LISSON. A MONTH BEFORE HE WENT MISSING. HIS FIRST WITHOUT MUM.

HOLD ON. THERE USED TO BE A MAP ON THIS WALL, OF THE WHOLE SURFACE OF TITAN.

OH, GOD. THIS ARRANGEMENT IS A MESSAGE... FROM DAD.

HOW DID YOU KNOW ITS LOCATION? YOU ARE CONCEALING INFORMATION.

I JUST KNEW, OKAY? AND NOW I KNOW.

WHAT IS IT YOU CLAIM TO KNOW?

THAT HE'S DEAD.

ALL OF THESE SITES HAVE ASSOCIATED PINHOLES, EXCEPT DRILL SITE SIERRA.

SO A PIN MEANS: "I WENT HERE".

ARE YOU PICTURING IT? IMAGINING?

I DON'T IMAGINE. THERE IS ANOTHER HOLE. HERE. "XANADU REGION".

HE WENT HERE. BUT HE DIDN'T MARK IT. WHY?

THAT'S WAY OUT. NO ONE'S DRILLING OUT THERE. THERE'S NOTHING THERE.

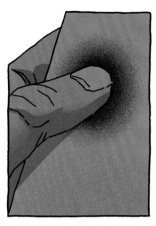

HEY!
HE HID IT
FOR ME!

IT NEEDS TO
STAY HIDDEN.

BASTARD!

DON'T
SCAN
ME.

XANADU IS
3 HOURS IN
THE AIR.

LET'S
MOVE.

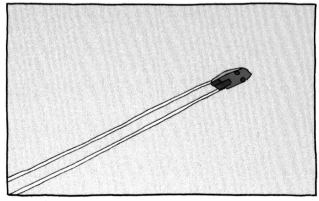

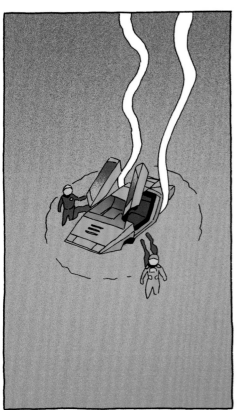

55

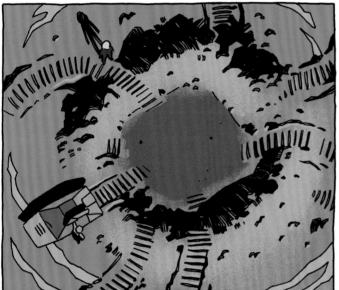

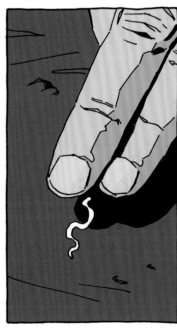

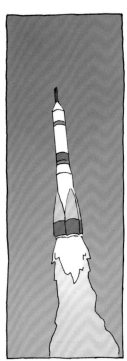

TAGGART...
HE'S...

HE'S
WHAT?!

HE'S
HERE.

The Lancet
March 2335
Editorial

# The Sleeper Science

Deep Space Psychosis Syndrome (DSPsS) is an ICD-22 diagnosis for an etiologically specific but mechanistically undefined space psychosis relating to Deep Space/Deep Time (DSDT) travel, the former relating to distance of travel and the latter relating to time of travel. First described in the mid-23rd century (Vishwanathan et al., 2265) during the burgeoning Deep Space movements of that period following the construction of ripple drive systems for DSDT travel, the syndrome required new instrumentation and terminology to be added to the ICD mechanism (ICD-20) in order to allow it to adequately describe this newly arising DSDT psychiatric condition. DSPsS underwent extensive study by both civilian and military institutions, but in the absence of a clear mechanism, and following the 7,412 deaths of DSDT travellers, all DSDT movement was subsequently banned in 2280. There has not been a case formally reported in the literature since the ban. There has also been a fall-off in clinical and laboratory reporting in this field since the late 23rd century (Martens et al., 2329). The subsequent collapse of the deep space economy is well documented.

The key symptomatology of Primary DSPsS was a hyperawareness within REM dreaming, with extreme and distressing distortion of the subjective experience of time. The symptom had two primary features. Firstly, upon dream recall, patients reported the clear, subjective knowledge within the dream that the dream would not end. Secondarily, and most perilously, patients reported that the dreams themselves were, in all 7,412 diagnosed individuals, terrifying in nature. Taken together, these symptoms led patients to experience Terror Dreams, what have been termed "a terror of timelessness" (Yeung et al. 2267) in which each patient apparently experiences extreme fear for a period subjectively reported to approach many hundreds of years. No single clinical identifier was detected in relation to the subjective perception of terror over seemingly unending time, but clearly the symptom, reported in isolation by 100% of Deep Space returners, was associated with significant morbidity in this cohort (Vishwanathan et al., 2265). This catastrophic fracturing of the dream cycle led to patients refusing sleep, and 99.8% of cases (7,398 out of 7,412) death occurred from suicide, the others occurring from REM-phase cardiac failure (Hano et al 2278).

There is no observable lesion on neurological examination, investigation or neuromapping of DSPsS patients. Other conditions are known to cause disruption to the process of dream recall, Charcot–Wilbrand Syndrome (Murri et al., 1984), and to dream narrative generation, Kelsey–Lightfoot Syndrome (Hargreaves et al., 2041), but these conditions do not appear to share an observable mechanism with DSPsS in which there are essentially no investigative findings on imaging or cellularneuromapping, and post-mortem investigations reveal normal brain morphology in 100% of patients (Ali et al., 2270).

In the absence of neurophysical and -anatomical correlates to DSPsS, the nature of the subjective experience remains unclear and undefined: unlike dreams themselves, the experience as described to clinicians and researchers evades empathetic capture, but has subsequently been named "The Darkness of Deep Space" in what might be termed the "social mythology" surrounding this condition. There is very little ongoing research and analysis on this syndrome but an increasingly cultish social milieu thrives, justifying the inclusion here of the observation that there have been reports of people undergoing illegal DSDT travel to elicit the experience recreationally (Lynn et al. 2291), but those individuals never returned to Earth. And there is, of course, the enduring myth of The Sleeper: the individual somehow able to sleep without experiencing Terror Dreams, and therefore able to DSDT travel. The anecdotal and, in the case of The Sleeper Mythology, factitious nature of these strands of the history of DSPsS push them beyond the scope or interest of formal literature review, but we note that the syndrome spans both clinical science and social folklore, and as such the findings of Davidson et al. presented in this issue present the intriguing possibility of articulation between the two.

Twelve months ago, following the declassification of 50-year-old materials from the archives of the United States Department of Deep Space, heavily redacted documented evidence has come to light of trials of a highly selective and experimental-stage bilateral occipitotemporal decerebration process. These documents, released online following anonymised freedom of information requests made to the US Government (www.sleeperleaker.com.ea/readme), are presented and scrutinised in this issue of The Lancet, with a concurrent partial anatomical and functional analysis of the processes contained within the documents (Davidson et al. 2335).

The observations this group make are startling. Redaction of the content makes full analysis impossible but Davidson and her team draw together three other key findings from the evidence base around DSPsS (Yeung et al. 2267; Marshall et al. 2268; Powell et al. 2289) to draw a triangulated conclusion that this decerebration process was designed to dislocate the mechanism of timeless terror dreaming from the consciousness/perception axis in the brains of the individuals who underwent this experimental process. Furthermore, they postulate the anatomical location of that mechanistic process, possibly the site of the invisible lesion in DSPsS, but redaction prevents further clarity as to the nature of the mechanism, if indeed the mechanism is known. What they finally postulate is that the result of such dislocation might be a cessation of the Terror Dreams following DSDT travel, opening up the possibility that individuals treated in this way may be able to travel safely in Deep Space/Deep Time.

(Full article Davidson et al., The Lancet, 2335: 451-502)

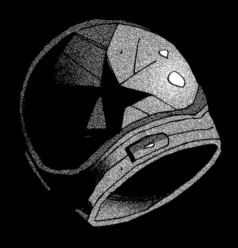

**CHAPTER 4**

WHOA.

OBS ARE SPIKING, COLONEL.

I'VE NEVER SEEN A SLEEPER DO THIS...

IN THE RED, HEART RATE'S KNOCKING 200!

161

HE'S DE-PRIMING.

THE TECH'S DECOUPLING SOMEHOW. I'M NOT SURE WHAT I'M READING HERE BUT IT LOOKS LIKE SOME KIND OF PRIMARY INTERFACE RUPTURE...

MARK 3 UNITS DON'T DE-PRIME, COLONEL, THEY CAN'T. THEY'RE GENOME-HARDWIRED.

BUT IF HE IS...

THIS IS COLONEL GHAVRI. I NEED THE PRE-PRIME REPORT ON DS-5, RIGHT NOW.

PRE-PRIME REPORT NUMBER DSPH-5/ALPHA CHARLIE ECHO ECHO LIMA FIVE NINER FOXTROT.

FILE IS AUTHENTIC.

HOUSTON P.D. VICE COP... OKAY... WHO WERE YOU, DS-5.

JESUS.

TRIED OUT FOR THE COWBOYS...

THANKS QUINN, YOU'RE DISMISSED.

I STAY WITH THE FILE, COLONEL. WOAH...

IS THAT... SHIT. I'D VOLUNTEER FOR PRIMING TOO.

COME WITH THE FILE.

DE-PRIMING? WHAT DOES THAT MEAN?!

REVERTING TO HUMAN.

SO HAND INVESTIGATIVE JURISDICTION TO THE TITAN SHERIFF DEPARTMENT WHERE IT SHOULD HAVE REMAINED, AND—

SENATOR, 79 YEARS AGO A MARK 1 SLEEPER DE-PRIMED. SHE KILLED 49 RESEARCH SCIENTISTS AND LEVELLED A 4-BLOCK RADIUS OF BUILDINGS AT ANNAPOLIS NAVAL BASE BEFORE THEY TOOK HER DOWN.

A DEPRIMED SLEEPER - WE THINK - REGAINS ALL PRE-PRIME MEMORY. SOME TECH STILL WORKS BUT CONTROL IS IMPAIRED: THEY GO OFF THE LEASH...

I READ HIS FILE. TRUST ME SENATOR. WE DON'T WANT THIS ONE OFF THE LEASH.

WHAT'S THE PLAY?

WE HAVE NO ONE ELSE ON TITAN. I NEED TO PUT TITAN SHERIFF DEPARTMENT PERSONNEL IN HARM'S WAY TO BRING HIM IN.

PERMISSION DENIED. YOU WANTED JURISDICTION: YOU'VE GOT IT. IF MEMORY SERVES, THESE THINGS HAVE A REMOTE TERMINATE. IT... HE'S A BRAVE MAN, HE'S SERVED HIS PLANET... IT'S A TRAGEDY. ETC. BUT... YOUR SLEEPER, YOUR NECK.

SECURE COMMS TO TITAN. DEPUTY...

RECORDED MESSAGE—

BRYCE.

YES MA'AM. STANDARD 80 MINUTE DELAY.

DEPUTY BRYCE, THIS IS COLONEL REETU GHAVRI, AUTHORIZATION EPSILON THREE NINER...

...YOU ARE TASKED T//$$*7-CA-ND—^*@ND A DEEP SPACE PRIMED HUMAN DESI&&TON DS-5 DEPLOYED ON TITAN. LAST KN99N POS^^%VN XANADU BADLAND COORDINATES—

GOT YOU NOW, YOU SON OF A BITCH.

WORLD-TO-WORLD COMMUNICATIONS ARE DOWN. WHAT THE FUCK?!

SCREW COMMS. WE KNOW WHERE HE IS. XANADU BADLANDS, ORBIT SPEED.

63

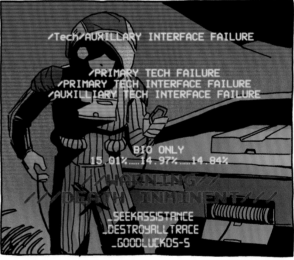

WAIT.

IF I DON'T REPORT IN... CUT THE CABLE. GET OFF-WORLD.

NO. YOU'RE SICK. I'LL GO. I'LL DO IT.

MAGIC HAND.

WHAT WAS THAT?

IT'S A 700-METRE CABLE. THEY NEVER DRILL ANYWHERE NEAR THIS DEEP. NOT ANY MORE.

THERE'S BEEN A MALFUNCTION IN THE SLEEPER.

GOOD MALFUNCTION? OR BAD MALFUNCTION?

TAKE "AUTONOMOUS" AND ADD "INCORRUPTIBLE".

WE CAN'T TAKE THE RISK.

FORTUNATELY, THE COLONEL AGREES.

SAYING AND DOING AREN'T THE SAME THING. I'VE GOT A GUY...

SAY AGAIN? HELLO?

FREEZE!

HANDS ABOVE YOUR HEAD!

THEY'VE FOUND US. THEY'VE FOUND US.

SHUT UP! WHERE IS HE?

...

"NEGLIGENT DISCHARGE. MY WEAPON BREACHED THE INTEGRITY OF HER EVA SUIT. IT WAS AN ACCIDENT..."

BE SMART.

YOU'RE NOT LAW ENFORCEMENT. WHO ARE YOU? WHO ARE YOU WORKING FOR?!

IS HE DOWN THERE?

I HAVE THE RIGHT TO REMAIN SILENT—

SLEEPER. DESIGNATION DS-5. THIS IS DEPUTY BRYCE, SHERIFF OF TITAN: YOU ARE INSTRUCTED TO MAKE YOURSELF KNOWN IMMEDIATELY. THERE'S NO WAY OUT, DS-5. I'VE GOT YOU.

THAT IS A MEASURABLE FACT.

FINE, WE'LL DO IT YOUR WAY, I'M HEREBY PLACING YOU UNDER ARREST AS AN ACCESSORY TO THE MURDER OF 83 CIVILIANS AND MILITARY PERSONNEL ON THE TITAN ORBITING STATION ISS HOUSTON. GET HER PROCESSED.

WE'RE GETTING A SIGNAL VIA THE JUPITER ARRAY. THERE'S NO NEW DATA FROM DS-5 IN THE INTERIM...

IN FACT... TITAN'S GONE SILENT.

ESTABLISHING A WORKAROUND.

DID MY TRANSMISSION TO DEPUTY BRYCE GET THROUGH? CHECK THE LOG...

COMMS ARE BACK UP! DUNNO HOW BUT WE'RE BACK...

DEPUTY BRYCE, TRANSMISSION FROM EARTH, SECURE CHANNEL, YOUR EARS ONLY.

WAIT!

68

Confirm active order.
Sleeper down.

IT'S TIME, SENATOR.

MADAM PRESIDENT, HONOURED GUESTS...

ON BEHALF OF THE DEPARTMENT OF DEEP SPACE, IT IS MY VERY GREAT PLEASURE TO WELCOME TO WASHINGTON OUR DISTINGUISHED COLLEAGUES FROM THE UNION OF KOREAN REPUBLICS, AND FURTHERMORE TO FORMALLY WELCOME THEM...

...TO THE TITAN GREEN PROJECT.

GO GREEN

GREEN COALITION WELCOMES KOREA

TAGGART

TAGGART

TAGGART

DOCTOR
MASSOUD
EL-BUSHRA.

TAGGART

YOU WERE
WRONG...

ABOUT WHAT?
ABOUT YOU?

ABOUT
TITAN GREEN?

**TO BE CONTINUED...**

# SKETCHBOOK